Jeanine Twigg's   Companion P

Embroidery Machine
ESSENTIALS

Fleece Techn

20 Designs with 85 Variations fo Embroidery on Fleece

By Nancy Cornwell

Published by

krause publications
700 East State Street • Iola, WI 54990-0001

Please call or write for our free catalog of publications. Our toll-free number, to place an order or to obtain a free catalog, is 800-258-0929. Please use our regular business telephone 715-445-2214 for editorial comment and further information.

ISBN: 0-87349-581-0

Project Manager: Jeanine Twigg
Illustrations and layout: Melinda Bylow
Design digitizing: Craig Dunmore

Table of Contents

Foreword

The Embroidery Machine Essentials: Companion Project Series was created to provide you with easy-to-stitch decorative designs and creative embroidery techniques to help develop your embroidery skills. Once you've had fun learning a variety of new ways to use these designs, you'll be able to use your personal design collection (and all the professionally digitized designs available to you) with an entirely new approach. Through the Companion Project Series you'll discover ways of looking beyond the "face value" of a design to recognize creative embroidery potential in every digitized design.

I've asked industry expert, Nancy Cornwell, who specializes in fleece, to show you some incredibly easy ways to mix embroidery with fleece. She has created some wonderful embroidery designs that can be used with a variety of creative fleece techniques. Nancy's techniques can be achieved with the simplest of designs... or parts of designs. It is with great pleasure that I introduce to you Fleece Techniques with famed author, Nancy Cornwell!

Jeanine

Introduction

When I wrote my second book, *More Polarfleece® Adventures*, I devoted a lot of attention to surface embellishment. I presented subtle accents to add interest and personality to fleece. In many ways, I was using my conventional sewing machine to mimic embroidery machine techniques.

Between the built-in capabilities of embroidery machines and the variety of embroidery designs available, it's fun to explore what happens when we use bits and pieces of designs to create entirely new designs and effects. Throughout the pages of this book I'll show you how to look at embroidery designs not only "as intended," but for all the opportunities each design offers for fleece embellishment.

All the designs included on the CD have designs within designs that represent a variety of fleece techniques. Each design will be shown fully stitched. Then, I'll uncover the "hidden designs" by picturing alternative ways to use the motifs. We'll be using parts and parcels of designs to create surface interest with a variety of trapunto effects, "embossing," and terrific new ways to take advantage of embroidery and fleece for easy appliqué. It's my objective to show you how to find the "hidden designs" that can be found within most embroidery designs available to you.

They say a picture is worth a thousand words, so you'll find yourself referring to the pictures more than the words to understand the end result of a technique. The techniques and design variations featured can be accomplished on your embroidery machine without additional software. Of course, if you add customizing, stitch editing, sizing, or digitizing to your machine's capabilities, your options multiply exponentially.

Fleece offers a tremendous canvas for embroidery creativity... hold on and get ready for another fun fleece adventure!

Nancy Cornwell

Nancy's Fleece Resource:

The designs in this book have been embroidered on Nordic™ Fleece manufactured by David Textiles, Inc. I have chosen this fleece because I can count on its consistent high quality and the fact that it is readily available to all fabric stores. If your local fabric store does not carry Nordic™ fleece, ask the owner or manager to order it.

Chapter 1
Embroidery Essentials

ou'll need to know this very important information <u>before</u> beginning your fleece embroidery adventure!!

Please don't skip this chapter and assume it is information you already know. You'll need this information to ensure successful embroidery, because most embroidery designs are geared towards woven fabric and we're working on stretchy, lofted fleece. Refer to this chapter often.

I'm assuming that you already have some embroidery experience and practice the embroidery "basics." It is important that you already know the importance of proper stabilization, appropriate needle, and test stitching. If you need more information, or a refresher on the "basics" refer to Jeanine Twigg's book, *Embroidery Machine Essentials*. Fleece is not tricky to embroider on, but knowing the "basics" will help you with these specialty techniques.

Embroidery Designs

The embroidery designs featured in this book are located on a CD-ROM on the inside back cover. The designs are specifically digitized to my specifications with more stops than a standard design, a variety of stitch lengths and an assortment of stitch densities to achieve certain surface effects on fleece. Each stop is considered a "segment" of the design.

Each design, along with all the individual segments, is pictured in the back of the book and on the CD. Be sure to print out the segment files from the CD and use them as a reference tool for motif placement and to help you visualize the various elements.

Designs purchased from other companies or the designs you currently own, may not stitch out in this same manner. My intent is to show you, by the arrangement of details, what elements to look for so that you may use other designs in a similar way.

All the designs on the CD include a perimeter baste as the first segment of the design. This helpful feature anchors the fleece and discourages fabric shifting during the embroidery process. Unless noted otherwise, the perimeter baste is always the first step of stitching a design.

As you examine other designs you already own, you may want to consider adding this perimeter

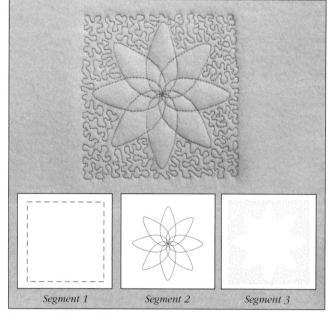

Sample of Stippled Flower and stitch segments

basting stitch into your embroidery process. Depending upon your embroidery machine it may be a built-in feature, or you may need to add this feature into a design with the aid of embroidery software. If your machine does not have the ability to perimeter baste the design area, use a temporary spray adhesive or baste by hand (if an adhesive would not be appropriate for a particular technique).

Each design is first shown stitched out complete, "as intended." Then, we will dissect each design to see what elements it offers and how we can use them. As we take apart the designs, we will "fast forward" through the stitches and skip segments of the design. Refer to your machine manual to see how to do this on your machine.

If your machine has the ability to turn the Stop "ON" and "OFF" (for monochromatic designs), make sure the Stop feature is "ON" so the machine will stop between segments.

As we dissect designs to use for various fleece techniques, we are not customizing or editing. All the techniques can be accomplished on your embroidery machine without assistance from software programs. However, if desired, you can always turn to your embroidery software to aid with the design dissection.

When extracting "hidden designs" in a design

you already own, you may have to manually stop the machine in the middle of a stitching sequence to achieve a particular technique. Carefully watch the needle as it progresses through the stitching and stop the machine at the desired place in the motif. In this method, there will not be a digitized "stop and tie-off." Therefore, leave thread tails long enough to pull to the wrong side and tie in a knot in order to prevent the design from unraveling.

IMPORTANT NOTE:
> *When using only a portion of a satin or fill stitch design, it is important to include the supporting stitches, too. Study the design and stitch the outline, zigzag and underlay stitches that will provide the foundation for the segments you are stitching.*

Embroidery on Fleece

Because fleece is lofty and has stretch, choose designs with lower stitch counts and less intricacy. Dense designs, with high stitch counts, are too heavy for the soft hand of fleece and they tend to distort the fabric. In designs with dense stitching, we will bypass certain steps to simplify the design. If a dense design offers a perfect look for fleece, I recommend adding extra layers of a lightweight cut-away stabilizer to achieve the desired results.

Use a specialty embroidery presser foot designed to accommodate bulky fabrics if one is available for your machine. Some techniques involve multiple fleece layers. If the layers tend to shift, reduce the pressure on the presser foot. Check your machine manual for this feature.

Test-Stitching

Always test-stitch a design, technique or segment (with the same stabilizer, thread, etc.), before stitching on the real project. This test will show if you need to add more stabilizer layers (for proper design alignment or stitch count), add or change a topping (for better thread coverage), or make machine adjustments (for prettier stitching).

If you are unsure how to correct a problem that shows up in the test-stitching process, refer to the in-depth Troubleshooting section in Jeanine Twigg's book, *Embroidery Machine Essentials*.

Stabilizers

There's not one "right stabilizer." The right stabilizer for your project is one that offers enough stability to allow your design to stitch out well combined with your personal taste.

For most fleece embroidery choose a soft, cut-away stabilizer under the fleece. A cut-away stabilizer is permanent and it remains an integral part of the design, which is necessary to maintain the motif shape and stitch integrity. A soft cut-away stabilizer will not interfere with the soft hand of fleece.

A topping is a stabilizer, too. It is used on top of the fleece and acts as a layer between the embroidery threads and the nap of the fleece. With fill-stitch designs, toppings are often necessary to prevent the fabric nap from interfering with the thread coverage. I am not addressing the use of toppings in general, because most of the time we are not using the fill stitch elements of a design on fleece. Occasionally, I suggest the use of a water-soluble topping depending on the fleece technique. For more information on toppings and their uses, refer to Jeanine Twigg's book, *Embroidery Machine Essentials* or my book, *More Polarfleece® Adventures*.

My Choice: I generally use a soft, mesh stabilizer on the underside of my fleece.

Temporary Spray Adhesives

If you choose to use a temporary spray adhesive for these fleece techniques, use it to adhere the fleece to the hooped stabilizer and the appliqué pieces to the base fleece. Always spray what is being adhered to the fleece rather than spraying directly onto the base fleece. Be sure to spray away from the embroidery machine as the over spray is harmful to your embroidery equipment.

For appliqué fabrics, lightly spray the adhesive onto the wrong side of the appliqué fabric and adhere it in place. Do not be heavy-handed with the spray as you'll need to trim the excess fabric away and won't want to contend with a strong adhesion. When possible, the perimeter baste (segment 1) is preferable over an adhesive spray.

If you use a temporary spray adhesive with a water-soluble stabilizer on the fleece, carefully read the directions for your chosen adhesive before rinsing. If it is a water-soluble adhesive, then you can rinse the fleece immediately. If it is not water-soluble, wait the recommended time for the spray to dissipate before rinsing the fleece.

Appliqué Scissors

While I have an arsenal of different scissor types, I use duckbill shaped appliqué scissors exclusively for trimming my fleece. The beveled edge and accurate points result in a clean blunt edge finish.

Spectacular Blanket (page 42)

Needles & Threads

The designs were digitized to accommodate a 40-weight high sheen thread. Choose a 75/11, 80/12, or 90/14 embroidery needle to accommodate the weight of the fleece. If you choose a different thread, change the needle and make any machine adjustments as dictated by your test-stitch sample. When using metallic threads, keep in mind that not all metallic threads behave the same. If you have difficulty with one thread, try a different brand. Be sure to use a 90/14 metallic needle.

Double needles are great when used with outline stitches. Your first thought might be that a double needle and embroidery aren't compatible, but in the proper setting, the results are great! Since it is the hoop that moves and not the needle, the only criteria to consider is whether the lines of the design will be enhanced with a double row of stitching. A 3.0 double needle gives very nice results on fleece. Make sure the double needle fits within the opening of your presser foot. Check with your embroidery machine dealer to determine if a double needle can be used with your embroidery equipment.

Hooping

Do not hoop the fleece. I prefer to hoop the stabilizer and use a perimeter baste or spray the stabilizer with adhesive to attach the fleece to the stabilizer. Fleece is stretchy, bulky, and awkward to hoop properly. In addition, hooping the fleece risks leaving an imprint of the hoop (hoop burn) in the fleece nap.

Fleece is a lofted, stretch fabric requiring different hooping techniques as noted in the instructions throughout the book. Consider using these techniques when stitching on other lofted and stretch fabrics.

The 'right' side of fleece

How do you to tell the right from the wrong side of fleece? Fleece will curl toward the <u>wrong</u> side when pulled on the cut edge (the direction of the most stretch). Fleece is always used with the right side facing up unless otherwise noted.

Embroidery Terms

Here are a few embroidery terms specific to this book. These terms will help you as you work through the instructions. For a comprehensive listing of embroidery terms refer to Jeanine Twigg's book *Embroidery Machine Essentials*.

Base fleece: The main item (garment, blanket, scarf, pillow top) that you are going to embroider.

Hidden Designs: An element or combination of elements extracted from an original design that result in a new motif. They are the whole purpose of the book!

Segments: A series of stitches that can be extracted from a design. It may be a design outline, a satin stitch edge finish, an inner motif accent, the underlay, etc. I have termed the series of stitches as "segments" within each design.

A Great Idea!

As you work through designs either from the CD or one of your own, keep a notebook alongside your machine. Make notes of start and stop points of design segments, variations that might look great stitched alone, quirks in a particular design, test-stitching results, and anything you want to remember for future projects. Keep adding to the notebook listing each design name and information. Over time you'll find the notebook has grown into quite a comprehensive reference guide. As you tackle new projects, you'll appreciate the wealth of information kept in the pages of the notebook and knowing that much of the preliminary work has already been done!

Chapter 2
Adventures With Appliqué Techniques

Traditional embroidery machine appliqué involves overlaying the base fabric with a woven appliqué fabric, an outline stitching of the motif, the trimming away of the excess appliqué fabric, and the satin stitch finish of the trimmed fabric edges. For the Stylized Flower, although we are using fleece as the base fabric, it is still considered "traditional appliqué" because we are using a woven appliqué fabric.

Stylized Flower

Although this design is simple, it provides a dramatic illustration of the potential any appliqué design has to offer.

Traditional Appliqué

Instructions:

1. Hoop a soft, cut-away stabilizer. Lightly spray the stabilizer with temporary spray adhesive and adhere the base fleece in position. (Why not hoop the fleece? Refer to "Hooping" on page 7.)

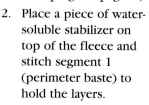

2. Place a piece of water-soluble stabilizer on top of the fleece and stitch segment 1 (perimeter baste) to hold the layers.

3. Cut a piece of cotton appliqué fabric for the leaves larger than the finished leaf area. Lightly spray temporary adhesive onto the wrong side of the appliqué fabric and adhere it in place.

4. Stitch segment 2 (leaf outline).

5. Remove the hoop from the machine. Do not remove the fabric from the hoop! Using appliqué scissors, trim the excess fabric close to the stitching line.

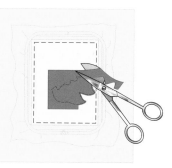

6. Return the hoop to the machine. Stitch segment 3 (leaf satin stitch) and segment 4 (vein detail).

7. Cut a piece of cotton appliqué fabric for the flower larger than the finished flower area. Lightly spray temporary adhesive onto the wrong side of the appliqué fabric and adhere it onto the base fleece.

8. Stitch segment 5 (flower outline).

9. Remove the hoop from the machine. Do not remove the fabric from the hoop! Using appliqué scissors, trim excess flower appliqué fabric close to the stitching line.

10. Return the hoop to the machine. Stitch segment 6 (flower satin stitch) and segments 7 and 8 (inner flower detail).

TIP:

In Jeanine's Basic Techniques *book, she recommends placing a layer of water-soluble stabilizer between the base fabric and the appliqué fabric. The water-soluble stabilizer keeps the fleece nap from pushing against the cotton appliqué fabric, which could interfere with the finishing satin stitches securing the appliqué. When trimming the appliqué piece, the stabilizer prevents inadvertent gouges of the base fleece nap. It may be necessary to "crispen" some water-soluble stabilizers for easier removal from the completed motif. (To "crispen," leave the stabilizer exposed to air to stiffen it a little.)*

Blunt Edge Appliqué

Traditional Appliqué with a cotton fabric may not be successful on high-loft thick fleece. The depth of the fleece narrows the satin stitch and may cause it to not adequately secure the appliqué. Be gentle! Handle the appliqué fabric gently when trimming. You risk misalignment of the satin stitches if the fabric shifts in the hoop.

For additional appliqué information and ideas refer to Jeanine Twigg's *Embroidery Machine Essentials* and her *Basic Techniques* books.

What happens if we use fleece as the appliqué material, but not the satin stitch edge finish? We have an appliqué with simplicity and depth. Overlay the fleece appliqué fabric for the leaves; stitch segments 2 and 4 (leaf outline and veins), and trim excess. Overlay the fleece appliqué fabric for the flower; stitch segments 5, 7, and 8 (flower outline and inner detail), and trim the excess. For more information, refer to the Blunt Edge Appliqué instructions (Rocking Horse) on page 10.

Fleece Appliqué

Look what else this design has to offer when we change the appliqué fabric, skip a couple of segments, add a bit of stuffing, and more. We generally start by hooping the stabilizer and adhering the fleece, but that's about the only thing that remains the same!

Let's repeat the above basic appliqué sequence using fleece as the appliqué fabrics. The added bulk of two fleece layers in the motif area combined with the sunken stitches of the inner flower and leaf detailing area gives tremendous dimension to the flower.

Textured

Eliminate the appliqué pieces and just stitch any or all of the design lines. Choose a contrasting thread color to make the motif noticeable, or a tonal color for subtle texture. If abstract subtlety is your style, try stitching only segment 5 (flower outline). To make this abstract splash a bit more noticeable, use two strands of thread through the needle. Use a larger needle (size 90/14 or 100/16) to accommodate the two threads.

Trapunto

Want a bit more dimension to your stylized flower? Try Trapunto! Stitch segment 2 (leaf outline) and 5 (flower outline) onto the base fleece and insert some stuffing between the stabilizer and the fleece. Finish with segment 4 (leaf veins) and segments 7 and 8 (inner flower details). Be sure to change to a larger needle before stitching over the stuffing. For more information, refer to the Trapunto instructions (Southwest Star) on page 18.

Dimensional Appliqué

Dimensional appliqué offers a raised surface embellishment. Let your machine do most of the work for you! For more information, refer to the Dimensional Appliqué instructions (Nested Flower) on page 25 for how to make the dimensional appliqué piece. Then, construct the flower using the following instructions.

Instructions:

1. Hoop a soft, cut-away stabilizer. Lightly spray the stabilizer with temporary adhesive and adhere the base fleece in position.

2. Using thread that matches the fleece, stitch segment 5 (flower outline).

3. Lightly spray temporary adhesive on the wrong side of the fleece flower appliqué.

4. Using the stitched flower outline as a placement guide, adhere the appliqué in place.

5. Secure the flower to the base fleece by stitching segments 7 and 8 (inner flower details).

Rocking Horse

Any design that offers uncomplicated outline stitches is perfect for an easy "cheater's" way to appliqué! Because fleece does not ravel, we can use this characteristic to our advantage. The results offer a soft padded appearance to the design.

Blunt Edge Appliqué

Blunt edge appliqué is exactly as the name implies. There are no finishing stitches over the edge of the appliqué. The neatly trimmed cut edge of the fleece is the finished edge of the appliqué!

When deciding which embroidery designs are suitable for blunt edge appliqué, look for simple shapes that are easy to trim, and designs that offer a simple outline stitching of the motif at some point in the order of stitching.

Instructions:

1. Hoop a soft, cut-away stabilizer. Lightly spray the stabilizer with temporary adhesive and adhere the base fleece in position.

2. Cut a piece of fleece appliqué fabric larger than the finished rocking horse area. Place the wrong side against base fleece and stitch segment 1 (perimeter baste).

3. Stitch the Rocking Horse motif through both fleece layers and stabilizer.

4. Using appliqué scissors, trim excess fleece appliqué fabric close to the stitching lines. Angle the scissors to give a clean crisp cut edge and be careful not to gouge the base fleece.

> **TIP:**
>
> *If you were applying a blunt edge fleece appliqué onto an item where the trimmed stabilizer on the wrong side would be visible (like a scarf or blanket) you may eliminate the stabilizer and directly hoop the base fleece. Since designs suitable for blunt edge appliqué are simplistic and with a lower stitch count, there is little danger of distorting the fleece. When hooping the fleece, hoop "lightly" to prevent hoop burn on the fleece nap.*

> **TIP:**
>
> *When using designs you already own for this technique and if your machine does not have a perimeter baste function, then lightly spray temporary adhesive onto the wrong side of the fleece appliqué and adhere it in place. Do not be heavy-handed with the adhesive. You will not want to contend with a strong adhesion as you trim the excess fabric. The perimeter baste, when available, is preferable over adhesive spray.*

Double-Sided Appliqué

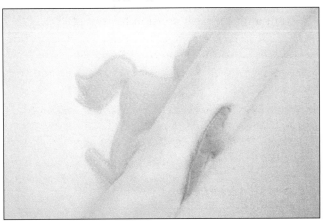

What's better than a Blunt Edge Appliqué? A double-sided Blunt Edge Appliqué! It's just like it sounds… an appliqué on both sides of the base fleece fabric. Perfect for blankets and scarves because you can embellish both sides of the fleece at the same time!

Although the Double-Sided Appliqué is not illustrated with every design throughout the book, just remember that if a design element works for Blunt Edge Appliqué it will also work for Double-Sided Appliqué.

Instructions:

1. Lightly hoop the base fleece.

2. Cut two pieces of fleece appliqué fabric larger than the finished the rocking horse area.

3. Place the wrong side of one fleece appliqué piece against the underside of the hooped base fleece. Place the wrong side of the second fleece appliqué piece on the top of the hooped base fleece.

Stitch segment 1 (perimeter baste). It is helpful to pin the layers together while you attach the hoop to the embroidery machine.

4. Stitch segment 2 (Rocking Horse).

5. Using appliqué scissors, trim the excess fabric close to the stitching lines on both sides of the base fleece.

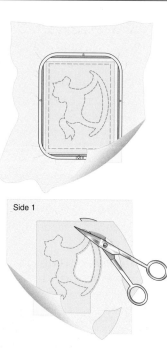

Side 1

TIP:
Hold the fleece layers in place while stitching the perimeter baste. Reduce the pressure on the presser foot if the layers tend to shift and your machine offers this capability.

Trapunto

Just like the Stylized Flower, the Rocking Horse offers the same opportunity to add a little stuffing for dimension. Lightly spray the hooped stabilizer with temporary adhesive and adhere the base fleece. Stitch the Rocking Horse. Cut a slit in the stabilizer and insert a small amount of stuffing. Hand stitch the stabilizer slit closed. For more information, refer to Trapunto instructions (Southwest Star) on page 18.

Contemporary Cat
Reverse Appliqué

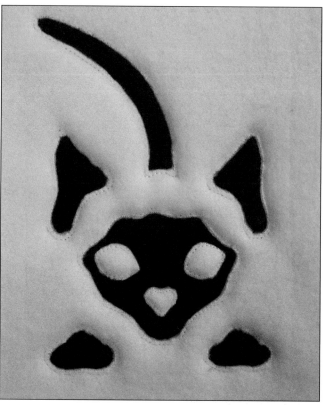

Reverse appliqué on fleece is quite similar to traditional reverse appliqué with woven fabrics... except quicker and easier. Because fleece does not ravel, we can eliminate the satin stitch finish!

When I created this cat design, more design elements were added than you would probably use in a reverse appliqué. However, the additional elements offer more creative use for this design. Pick and choose the elements according to what you are making and the look you want.

The reverse appliqué technique utilizes a double layer of contrasting fleece and a quick fabric trim. By trimming away the top layer within the motif stitching lines, the contrast fabric will be revealed. The two layers of fleece can be a base fleece (a garment) and a fleece appliqué, or a full double-layered fleece project (a blanket or scarf). The hooping and fabric arrangement for a garment will be different than the arrangement for a blanket.

Instructions (garment):

1. Hoop a soft, cutaway stabilizer. Spray with temporary adhesive and adhere the fleece appliqué fabric to the stabilizer right side facing up.

2. With the right side facing up, place the base fleece on top of the fleece appliqué and stitch segment 1 (perimeter baste).

3. Stitch segments 2, 3, and 4 (cat, eyes, and nose outlines).

4. Using appliqué scissors, trim away the top layer of the base fleece from within the stitched areas of the tail, ears, face, and paws to reveal the fleece appliqué layer peeking through. Leave the fleece double-layered inside the eyes and the nose.

Instructions (blanket or scarf):

1. Hoop a medium to heavyweight water-soluble stabilizer.

2. With wrong sides together and layers aligned, lay both fleece layers on the hooped stabilizer and stitch segment 1 (perimeter baste) to secure all the layers. (When using other designs — if you cannot machine baste, hand baste or pin fleece layers together. Lightly dampen the stabilizer with a sponge to make the stabilizer tacky and then adhere the fleece to the stabilizer.)

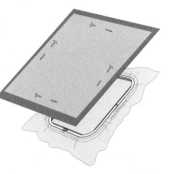

3. Stitch segments 2, 3, and 4 (cat, eyes, and nose outlines).

4. Tear-away or cut-away as much of the stabilizer as possible.

5. Using appliqué scissors, trim away the one layer of fleece from within the stitched areas of the tail, ears, face, and paws to reveal the contrast fleece peeking through. Leave the fleece double-layered inside the eyes and the nose.

6. Following the manufacturer's directions, thoroughly rinse to remove the remaining stabilizer.

Try using a pretty cotton print as the appliqué fabric under the fleece. Hoop stabilizer, lightly spray with temporary adhesive and adhere cotton print, right side facing up. Place the base fleece on top and stitch segment 1 (perimeter baste). Stitch segments 2, 3 and 4 (cat, eyes, and nose outline). Trim away inside of tail, face, ears, and paws to reveal the "calico cat." Do not trim inside the eyes or the nose. Finish with any segment facial features you desire.

This motif offers more mix-and-match combinations than we have the space to show. From simple blunt edge appliqué and double-sided appliqué, to just using parts and parcels of the cat — this design has a lot to offer. Referring to the Rocking Horse (for Blunt Edge and Double-Sided appliqué instructions) and the Reverse Appliqué instructions, consider these possibilities:

Blunt Edge Appliqué

Refer to the Blunt Edge instructions (Rocking Horse) on page 10 and then try these combinations of elements for a variety of effects:

Stitch segments 2, 3, and 4 (cat, eyes, and nose outlines) and trim out the eyes.

> **TIP:**
> To avoid excess handling of the hooped fleece and risk possible shifting of the fabric, after segment 2 trim the excess from only the lower face and upper paw area. Stitch the remaining elements and then finish the complete trim.

Use all the elements. With matching thread, stitch segment 2 (basic cat). Trim excess fleece appliqué from outer edges, leaving the tail, ears, face, and paws. With contrasting thread, stitch segments 3 through 9.

Stitch part of segment 2 (just the face and ears). Stitch left ear, fast forward past the tail, right ear, face, and stop. Leave threads tails to pull to the wrong side and manually tie off. Finish with as many of the added facial features as you like.

Textured

On a single layer of fleece and using two strands of contrasting thread through a larger size needle, stitch segments 2, 3, 4, 6, 8, and 9 (all the outline details). For subtle facial features, thread the needle with two of the same color threads and stitch segments 3, 4, 6, 8, and 9 (outline of eyes, nose, whiskers and mouth).

Crescent Moon & Star

Blanket Stitch Appliqué

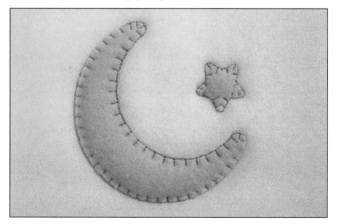

Appliqués with a hand-stitched look are charming. There are many embroidery designs that offer this look, but most will not work on fleece because the stitch width may be too narrow to securely catch the cut edge of a fleece appliqué.

The Crescent Moon & Star, however, were digitized for use on fleece. The design will work on woven fabric, too!

> **NOTE:**
> The instructions below are the "real way" to stitch this design. Personally for fleece, I would "cheat" and use the blunt edge appliqué technique (see page 10). It looks almost the same, is faster and easier, and removes the inherent variables (not to mention additional work) in making templates and cutting separate appliqué pieces. The Blunt Edge method would also allow you to use other designs that do not provide a wide enough bite for the "real way."

Instructions:

Blanket Stitch Appliqué uses a design template to cut out the appliqué shapes before stitching them in place.

1. Cut out fleece appliqué pieces by referring to Dimensional Appliqué instructions (Nested Flower) on page 25.

> **NOTE:**
> Unlike cutting an appliqué from woven fabric, cutting appliqué pieces from fleece brings many variables into the picture — thickness, nap, and stretch. This doesn't necessarily mean there will be a problem, it just means that accurate cutting and test-stitching is a "must."

2. Hoop a soft, cut-away stabilizer. Lightly spray the stabilizer with temporary adhesive and adhere the base fleece in position.

3. With thread matching the base fleece color, stitch segment 2 (motif outlines) as a guide for appliqué placement. Refer to Dimensional Appliqué (Stylized Flower) on page 10.

4. Spray temporary adhesive onto the wrong side of cut out fleece appliqués and adhere in position.

5. Stitch segment 3 (blanket stitch finish).

> **NOTE:**
> If your test-stitch resulted in the blanket-stitching not catching the appliqué pieces sufficiently, cut new appliqué pieces slightly larger and try again. This means the loft and stretch of the fleece interfered. Or... consider using the Blunt Edge "cheater" technique on page 16!

Even though the designs aren't necessarily hidden, you still have more options for using this versatile design.

Blunt Edge Appliqué

Looks like the "real thing," but much easier and quicker! Stitch segment 2 (motif outline) and trim the excess. Stitch segment 3 (blanket stitch). For more information, refer to Blunt Edge Appliqué instructions (Rocking Horse) on page 10.

Double-Sided Appliqué

Similar to the Blunt Edge variation above, this version results in a fleece appliqué on both the top

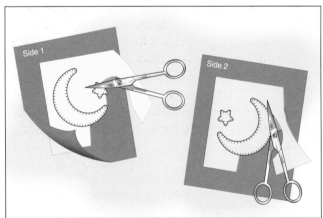

and underside of the base fleece. This is a great idea for embellishing both sides of a baby blanket in one easy step. For more information, refer to Double-Sided Appliqué instructions (Rocking Horse) on page 11.

Project Ideas

Freestanding Double-Sided Appliqué

As I looked at these motifs, the gentle shapes seemed perfect for a baby crib mobile, or an ornament for the Christmas tree. (This is a great idea to use with other blanket-stitched designs you already own.) This unique approach does not use a base fabric!

Instructions:

1. Hoop medium to heavy weight water-soluble stabilizer.
2. Lay two pieces of fleece appliqué fabric, wrong sides together on top of the stabilizer and stitch segment 1 (perimeter baste) to secure the layers. (When using other designs you own and if you cannot machine baste, pin or hand baste layers together, lightly dampen the stabilizer with a sponge to make the stabilizer tacky and adhere fleece.)
3. Stitch the entire design.
4. Trim the stabilizer and fleece layers close to the blanket-stitching lines. Remove as much of the water-soluble stabilizer as possible from within the stitching lines.
5. Following the manufacturer's directions, thoroughly rinse the fleece to remove remaining stabilizer.

> **IMPORTANT CAUTION:**
> *If you used spray adhesive, carefully read the directions for your chosen adhesive before rinsing. If it is a water-soluble adhesive, you can rinse immediately. If it is not, wait the recommended time for the spray to dissipate before rinsing.*

Temporary Cat

Want a great Halloween Black Cat garment…. but only for one day? Lightly hoop black fleece. Use an off-color thread stitch segment 2 (tail, ears, face, and paws). Remove fabric from hoop. Use the stitching lines as a guide to cut out the appliqué cat pieces. Spray the wrong side of appliqué pieces with a craft temporary appliqué adhesive and adhere black cat appliqué pieces to your garment. Peel off when finished. Be sure to test the adhesive before adhering the cat pieces to the garment.

Simple-to-Stitch Scarf

This scarf could have been embellished using a variety of designs. Shown here is a double layer scarf with Reverse Appliqué by trimming the cat on opposite sides at each end. As an alternative, use one layer of fleece and the Blunt Edge or Double-Sided Appliqué technique. You'll only need 1/4 to 1/3 yard of fleece to make this scarf. Refer to the Quick Fringe technique in *Polar Magic* for a "quick-as-a-wink" way to cut fringe.

Reversible Blanket

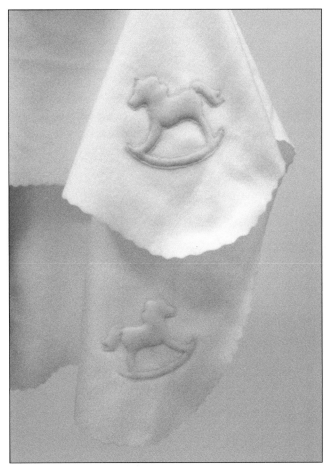

There's no right or wrong side to this blanket when the Rocking Horse is appliquéd on both sides! This is the perfect gift for a baby shower or a new mom. Everyone will wonder how you aligned the Rocking Horse on both sides so perfectly. And, you'll be the only one who'll know it was embroidered in one easy, double-sided appliqué step! The wave blade rotary cutter creates the perfect edge finish.

Chapter 3
Adventures With Quilting Techniques

Charming motifs with subtle stitches have been part of the quilting world for generations. Embroidery machines can duplicate the look of quilting and provides an alternative for hand stitching. But, don't limit the use of quilting designs to just traditional applications. The simplicity and openness of quilting designs lend themselves beautifully for use on fleece, offering a wonderful opportunity for subtle texture and surface interest.

Southwest Star

The Southwest Star is an excellent design to stitch "as intended" for subtle texture. But, add a bit of stuffing for Trapunto, or use the star or the chevron alone. The solitary star can even double as a snowflake!

Trapunto

Instructions:

1. Hoop a soft, cut-away stabilizer. Place the base fleece on top of the stabilizer and stitch segment 1 (perimeter baste).

2. Stitch the motif.

3. Remove the fabric from the hoop and trim the stabilizer 1/4" away from the stitching lines.

> **CAUTION:**
> *Do not trim the stabilizer too closely as the stuffing can exert pressure on the stitching lines.*

4. To "plump" the star portion of the motif, cut a slit in the stabilizer and insert stuffing. Hand stitch the opening closed. Note: If spray adhesive was used, insert a blunt tip instrument (like a stylus or the wrong end of a crochet hook) into the slit to separate the layers before inserting the stuffing.

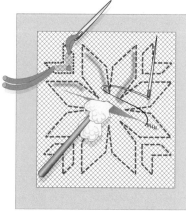

5. To "plump" the arrows, thread a large-eye tapestry needle with 4-ply acrylic yarn. Working from the wrong side, insert the needle in the stabilizer at one end of the arrow, slipping the needle between the stabilizer and the fleece. Exit the needle at the arrow point, pulling the double strand of yarn between the layers. Reinsert the needle in the exit hole (at the point) and exit the stabilizer at the other end. NOTE: Exiting and reinserting results in a nicer point than if you tried to feed the yarn all in one step.

6. Clip the yarn tails at the entrance and exit holes.

> **NOTE:**
> *When using other designs from your collection and your embroidery machine does not have the perimeter baste function, lightly spray the stabilizer with temporary spray adhesive and adhere the base fleece in position. Do not be heavy-handed because you will insert stuffing between the layers and do not want to contend with strong adhesion.*

STUFFING GUIDELINES: Use a small to moderate amount of stuffing when doing trapunto on a garment (so it doesn't look and feel like hard lumps) or when detail stitching will be sewn over it (the machine and needle need to be able to handle the bulk). You can insert more stuffing in home dec projects, like a pillow top or a blanket. Be careful with designs where the finishing stitches need to align with previous stitch lines. Stuff lightly to avoid misalignment.

Blunt Edge Appliqué

Stitch segment 2 (star). If you choose an icy winter fleece color, the star becomes a snowflake! For more information, refer to Blunt Edge Appliqué instructions (Rocking Horse) on page 10.

Reverse Appliqué

When using two layers of fleece, the reverse appliqué technique results in a recessed appearance compared to the subtle padded look of the blunt edge technique or the plump look of Trapunto. For a fun option, choose an appropriate cotton print as the underlayer and have a "printed star." If using a cotton print for the under layer, use pinking shears to trim the edges to inhibit raveling and consider interfacing the fabric prior to embroidery. For more information, refer to Reverse Appliqué instructions (Contemporary Cat) on page 12 and 13.

Design Manipulation

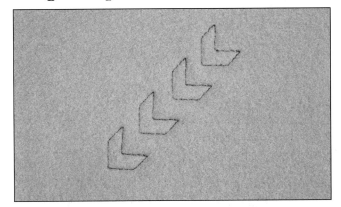

You can stitch segment 3 (the chevrons) and use them as a "frame accent" combined with other motifs or, as shown here, experiment a little by playing with just one chevron. You can apply this technique with any small single design element (bird, heart, flower, leaf, etc.). Depending upon your patience level, you can do quite a bit of creative maneuvering.

> **NOTE:**
> Some embroidery machines may offer the ability to single out one chevron and maneuver it in the hoop, but you won't know until you try! Patience and test stitching are important to figure out how to move and align the chevron on your particular machine. Some machines will allow you to move the hoop after you stitch the first chevron. Other machines will consider you to be "in the middle of a design" and not allow you to move the hoop unless you backtrack to the beginning of the design and pretend you are starting over.

Instructions:

Choose a large hoop. Even though we are using only a small part of the design, the machine recognizes the design as a full 4" X 4" motif. Changing to a larger hoop offers the ability to move the design outside the range of a standard size hoop.

1. Hoop a soft, cut-away stabilizer. Place the hoop on the machine.
2. Use the hoop movement arrows to move the design in the uppermost right corner of the hoop. Move the needle to the motif center and mark this position on the stabilizer.
3. Remove the hoop from the machine, spray the hooped stabilizer with temporary spray adhesive and adhere base fleece to the stabilizer using the center

mark as a guide for fabric placement. (You can print out full-sized designs from the CD for reference.)

4. Return the hoop to the machine and again mark the position of the needle, this time on the fabric.

5. Remove the hoop from the machine. Do not remove the fabric from the hoop! Mark the fabric with a 45-degree line extending down from the motif center. Mark three more "center marks" on the diagonal line, indicating the spacing you want for the next chevrons. (In the pictured sample, I used 1" spacing for the chevrons.)

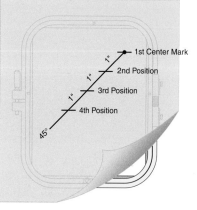

6. Stitch segment 3 (chevrons), stopping the machine as soon as the first chevron is tied off and before the second chevron starts to stitch.

7. Move the needle to the motif center position and move the hoop down to the next placement mark on the fleece.

8. Go back to the beginning of segment 3 (chevrons) and stitch the first chevron; again stopping before the second chevron begins stitching.

9. Repeat for the third and fourth chevrons.

Stippled Flower

Quilting designs, stitched "as intended," offer lovely texturing on fleece without making any alterations. This quilting design incorporates stippling stitches that provide added texture by contrasting the unstitched lofted areas with a high stitch compressed area.

Trapunto with Batting

The flower alone is a nice design for Trapunto. However, the insertion of stuffing into all the individual flower petals can be a lot of busy work. It is much easier to include batting in the stitching process.

Instructions:

1. Hoop a soft, cut-away stabilizer. Lightly spray the stabilizer with temporary adhesive and adhere a piece of low or medium loft batting.

2. Lightly spray the batting with temporary adhesive and adhere the fleece in place.

3. Stitch segment 1 (perimeter baste) and segment 2 (flower motif).

4. Trim the excess stabilizer and batting.

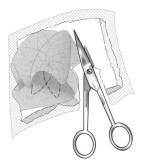

Trapunto

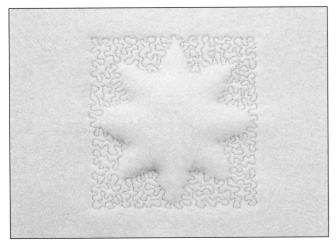

What a different look you can achieve when skipping the flower and using only the background stipple stitches! It is even more dramatic when stuffing the fleece for a trapunto effect. For more information, refer to Trapunto instructions (Southwest Star) on page 18.

Pinwheel Block

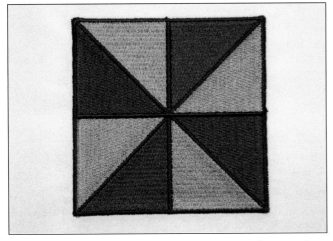

Theoretically, this design belongs in Chapter 5, but with its obvious quilting flavor, I decided to include it here.

Stitched "as intended," the Pinwheel Block is too compact with stitches to use on a fleece garment. A stabilizer (or layers of stabilizer) heavy enough to handle this motif, combined with the quantity of stitches used in this design would overpower the softness and drape of fleece. This design is intended for, and best suited for use on a woven fabric. However, that doesn't mean we can't take it apart and use parts and parcels of it for fleece. (Remember this thought when studying other designs in your personal design library.)

Reverse Appliqué

Want to make a quick "quilt"? Let your embroidery machine "quilt" for you! Stitch the "seamlines" and trim away specific areas to reveal a pinwheel quilt motif. Using two contrasting colors of fleece placed wrong sides together, stitch segment 2 (seam lines). On one side of the "quilt," use appliqué scissors to trim the top fleece layer from alternating triangles. On the other side of the quilt, trim the opposite triangles. For more information, refer to Reverse Appliqué instructions (Contemporary Cat) on page 12.

Textured

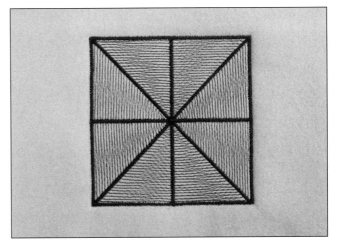

The purpose of underlay stitches is to provide a foundation for the satin or fill stitches that follow. Underlay stitches can appear random and non-specific, but sometimes the stitches may offer an interesting textural effect on fleece.

Stitch segments 3 and 5 (underlay stitches). Finish with segment 7 (satin stitch).

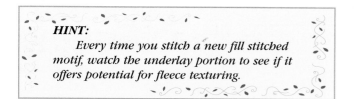

Trapunto

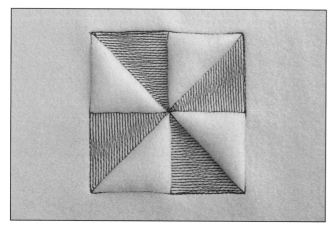

This would be a nice dimensional embellishment for a fleece pillow top or on a fleece garment.

Stitch segment 2 (outline) and segment 3 (underlay). Insert stuffing in the unstitched triangles. If using this as embellishment on a pillow top, and since there will be no additional stitches sewn over the stuffing, you can insert a little more stuffing than normal for more definitive dimension. For more information, refer to Trapunto instructions (Southwest Star) on page 18.

Project Idea

Elegant Pullover

A little bit of finesse went into this spectacular garment. Stitch three Stippled Flower motifs on the diagonal, frame the designs with two rows of double-needle pintucks on the sewing machine and you'll have an elegant fleece embellishment. The stippling stitches "emboss" the fleece and enhance the loft of the flower petals. The Polar Ribbing neck finish adds just the right designer touch.

Chapter 4
Adventures With Innovative Designs

The chapter titles for this book reflect the character or use of the designs. When I designed the motifs for this chapter, they didn't really fit into any particular classification, so that's why it's called "Adventures With Innovative Designs."

The purpose of this book is to look for all the different usable parts of a design so the concept of a "nested" group of shapes seemed quite logical. Each segment has a separate color to make it easy to pick and choose the size you want to use.

Nested Flowers

Every photograph of a Nested Flower technique represents six different flower sizes that can be stitched with a myriad of combinations!

All of the techniques shown with Nested Flowers will work beautifully with the Nested Hearts and Nested Stars, too.

Echo Effect

Simply stitch the design "as is." The design can be stitched on a single layer of fleece adhered to the stabilizer, or it can be stitched on a double layer of fleece resulting in more distinctive channels. Try stitching the design with monochromatic threads in graduated shades of your favorite color.

Blunt Edge Appliqué

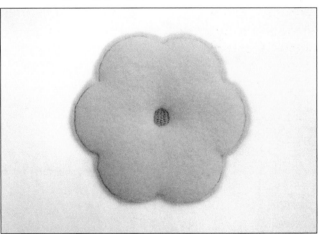

Stitch the flower size you want and finish with segments 8 and 9 (flower center). For more information, refer to the Blunt Edge Appliqué instructions (Rocking Horse) on page 10 and choose any or all of the flower sizes.

Optional: Attach a sport snap for the flower center.

Fun Idea

Apply a variety of flower sizes and fleece colors to the base fleece to make an all-over "flower print." Or, use your conventional sewing machine to satin stitch a meandering line and then "plant" blunt edge flower appliqués on the "vine." Be sure to use a tear-away stabilizer under the fleece as stabilization during the stitching.

Double-Sided Appliqué

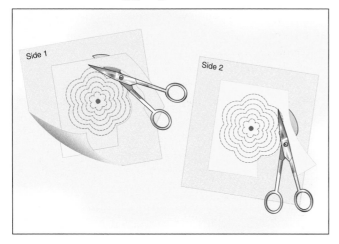

Here's a great accent for a scarf, blanket, or reversible vest. Use all the same color fleece flowers on one side of the vest and multi-colored fleece flowers on the other. For more information, refer to Double-Sided Appliqué instructions (Rocking Horse) on page 11.

Reverse Appliqué

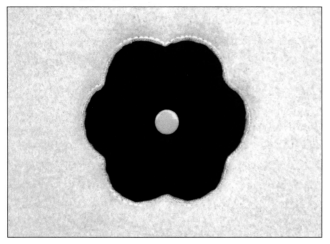

Anytime you have two layers of fleece you can have reverse appliqué. Leave the center plain or, as shown here, finish with a sport snap. For more information, refer to Reverse Appliqué instructions (Contemporary Cat) on page 12.

Trapunto

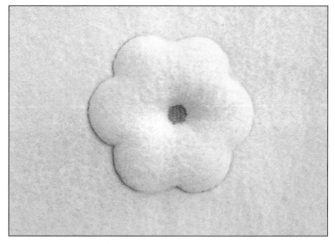

The simplicity of the flower outline is perfect for trapunto. Remember not to trim the stabilizer too closely to the stitching line since the stuffing will exert some pressure on the stitches. If finishing with the stitched flower center, do not overstuff. Change to a larger size needle for stitching the center. For more information, refer to Trapunto instructions (Southwest Star) on page 18.

Double Needle Embroidery

What happens when you use a double needle in your embroidery machine? You get a delicate ribbon-like stitching effect!

Your first thought might be that a double needle and embroidery aren't compatible, but in the proper setting, the results are great! Since it is the hoop that moves and not the needle, the only criteria to consider is whether the lines of the design will be enhanced with a double row of stitching. If in doubt, a test-stitching is worth the time to find out. A 3.0 double needle gives very nice results on fleece.

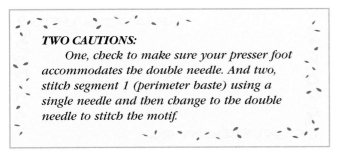

TWO CAUTIONS:
One, check to make sure your presser foot accommodates the double needle. And two, stitch segment 1 (perimeter baste) using a single needle and then change to the double needle to stitch the motif.

Interesting variation

Just like bobbin work offers interesting texture on the conventional sewing machine, look at the underside of double needle embroidery. Sometimes it looks like cross-stitch and with a smaller double needle, it looks like cording. You might just decide to occasionally embroider from the wrong side!

Dimensional Appliqué

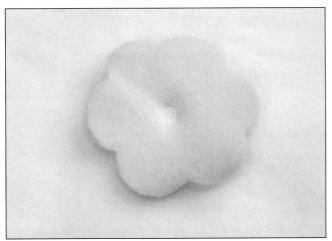

Does dimensional appliqué fascinate you? You can easily make your embroidery machine your partner in this adventure.

Instructions:

1. To make a separate appliqué piece, cut a piece of fleece appliqué fabric larger than your hoop. Lightly hoop the fabric.

2. Using an off-color thread (for visibility), stitch the outline of the chosen flower size. Bring the needle to the motif center and use a fabric marker to mark the flower center.

3. Unhoop the fabric and cut out the appliqué using the stitching line as a guide. Set the flower aside.

4. To attach the dimensional flower, hoop a soft, cut-away stabilizer. Lightly spray the stabilizer with temporary adhesive and adhere the base fleece in position.

5. Use the appropriate function on your machine to bring the needle to the center of the design.

6. Place the cut out flower appliqué under the presser foot, placing the marked flower center (from step 2) directly under the needle at the center motif position.

7. Stitch segments 8 and 9 (flower center).

Fun Idea

Add "inside petals" for a nice variation to the Dimensional Flower. This variation requires precise positioning of the dimensional flower so that the inner flower lines up perfectly. Follow the instructions above for making the separate appliqué piece, choosing any size flower except the smallest one (segment 2).

Refer to the Dimensional Appliqué instructions on page 10 for stitching the placement guide. Then, stitch segments 2, 8, and 9 (smallest flower and flower center) to secure the dimensional appliqué to the base fleece.

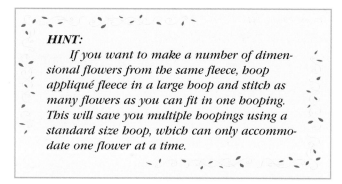

HINT:

If you want to make a number of dimensional flowers from the same fleece, hoop appliqué fleece in a large hoop and stitch as many flowers as you can fit in one hooping. This will save you multiple hoopings using a standard size hoop, which can only accommodate one flower at a time.

Chenille

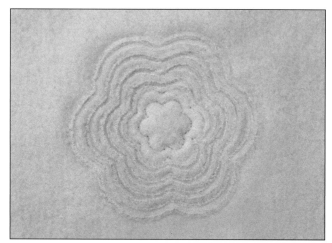

Anytime you have a series of narrow stitched channels, you have the opportunity for making fleece chenille. Traditionally, chenille is done by straight stitching multiple diagonal rows on multiple layers of woven fabric. The top layers are then slashed open leaving the bottom layer intact as the base. Either through laundering or using a brush, the cut edges are "roughed up" to encourage them to "bloom."

The theory of chenille is the same on fleece — just quicker and easier! We only need two layers of fleece in contrasting colors. As soon as the channels are slashed open, the tension from the sunken stitches is released and the fleece instantly "blooms!"

Choose designs that offer multiple rows of parallel stitching lines that will create channels wide enough to cut open with appliqué scissor tips but not wider than 3/8." Fleece chenille "blooms" best when done in narrow rows and on the bias. Straight-of-grain cuts, crossgrain cuts, and wide channel cuts tend to lay closed.

For best results:

- Choose two high-contrast colors of fleece. (Only a little of the under layer of fleece peeks through the slash opening, so subtlety would be lost.)
- Choose a design with a minimum of three channels to slash open.
- Choose a design where at least half or more of the cutting lines are on the bias.

Instructions:

1. Lightly spray a piece of hooped stabilizer with temporary adhesive spray and adhere the first fleece layer right side up. Note: If stabilizer would be visible in the finished project, lightly hoop the first layer of fleece instead of the stabilizer.

2. Place the second layer of fleece on top of the hooped fleece and stitch segment 1 (perimeter baste).

3. Stitch segments 2 through 9.

4. Using appliqué scissors, insert the scissor points into the top layer of fleece only, between stitching lines, and cut open the channels. Center the cutting lines between the stitching lines.

Chenille Blunt Edge Appliqué

The Chenille instructions remain the same, only the fleece arrangement changes. For chenille appliqué, consider this technique a version of Blunt Edge Appliqué. The fleece appliqué is placed on top of the base fleece and the motif is stitched. After cutting the top fleece layer between the stitching lines, trim the excess fleece appliqué close to outer edge of motif. For more information, refer to Blunt Edge Appliqué instructions (Rocking Horse) on page 10.

Nested Hearts

All of the techniques shown with the Nested Flowers apply to the Nested Hearts, too! Stitch each heart individually or all together with the same color thread to add fleece dimension to any project. In addition, the simplistic nature of this nested design can provide you with a variety of techniques in a single design.

Side-by-Side Hearts (Flowers or Stars, too!)

Stitch a row of hearts across a shirt front, down the center back of a jacket, across a pillow top, or at the end of a scarf. Use a large hoop to eliminate multiple hoopings. The all-in-one Nested Hearts will allow you the versatility to mix-and-match heart sizes.

Instructions:

1. Use a fabric marker to draw a line on the base fleece to mark the center for the heart row. (Across a sweatshirt front, down a center back or down a sleeve.)

2. Hoop a soft, cut-away stabilizer in a large hoop. Lightly spray with temporary adhesive and adhere the base fleece, centering the drawn line vertically in the large hoop.

3. Attach the hoop to the machine. Using the hoop movement arrows, move the design to the upper-most position. Bring the needle to the design center position and align it to the drawn line. Use a fabric marker to mark the position for "top" heart.

4. Repeat the above step to mark the lowest position.

5. Remove the hoop from the machine. Measure and center a third mark between the other two marks.

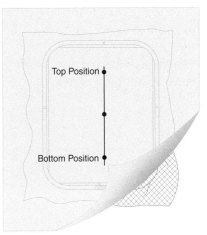

6. Determine the heart size desired and stitch the motifs, using the marks for placement. Be sure to rotate the hearts to stitch in the proper direction if necessary. To see the hearts sizes available, full-sized designs can be printed from the CD.

Nested Stars

All of the techniques shown with the Nested Flowers and Nested Hearts apply to the Nested Stars, too!

Frayed Patch

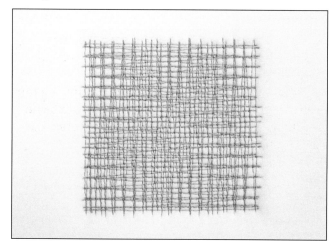

This design is not intended to be a "stand alone" motif, although it would be pretty sprinkled on a garment, in metallic or variegated threads. The Frayed Patch provides an interesting background on which other small to medium-sized motifs can be embroidered. Test the patch in one color, two colors, variegated thread, and metallic thread.

Here's a sample of the Frayed Patch with the Fern stitched with metallic thread — the perfect combination!

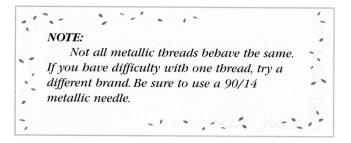

NOTE:
Not all metallic threads behave the same. If you have difficulty with one thread, try a different brand. Be sure to use a 90/14 metallic needle.

Textured Frame

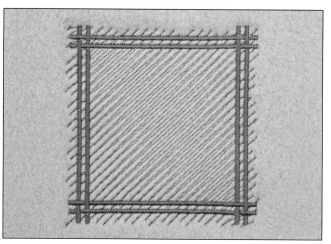

My favorite designs are the Framed Leaves shown starting on page 37. As I was working through the variety of options these designs had to offer, it suddenly struck me that having just a textured background, a frame, or both would be a terrific design to combine with other motifs.

Combining Designs

The combining of designs can be easily achieved, but the test-stitching of both designs to verify size is important. Before starting this combination, check to see if you can enlarge the frame using a standard size hoop. It may be necessary to change to a larger hoop to continue the designs.

Instructions:

1. Reduce the ladybug 20%.
2. Select the design segments to stitch and embroider the ladybug.
3. Load the Textured Frame onto your machine.
4. Enlarge the design 20%.
5. Stitch segment 1 (perimeter baste) to check the "fit."
6. Stitch segment 3 (the frame).

Fun Idea

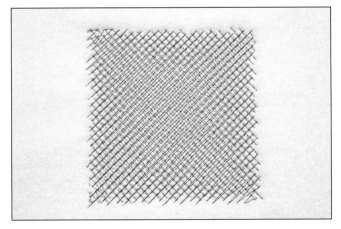

Use the background of the textured Frame to make a diagonally stitched Frayed Patch! Stitch segment 2 (background). Then mirror-image or rotate the design and stitch segment 2 again. It may be necessary to utilize a larger hoop to accommodate the design rotation or mirror-image function on your machine.

Project Idea

Starry Hat

Super simple to make, this crusher hat only uses a 1/4 yard of two fleece colors. The Nested Stars outline embroidered using the Reverse Appliqué technique on the crown compliments the embroidered motifs on the contrast roll back band. Directions for the construction of the Crusher Hat can be found in *Polar Magic*.

Chapter 5
Adventures With Traditional Designs

When I used to think of machine embroidery, I visualized a design full of stitches, threads blending colors, detail stitches adding accents, and perhaps an outline stitch defining the perimeter. It was like a photo in stitches.

Traditional embroidery designs usually stand alone. But, as we've explored in previous chapters, there are many more embellishment opportunities hidden within the designs.

All the designs in this chapter offer a multitude of technique options. We'll be extracting portions of the design we used in Blunt Edge Appliqué, Double-Sided Appliqué, Trapunto, and Texturing. But, in this chapter, the designs have more segments to play with, more details to fast-forward through, and more creative options to consider.

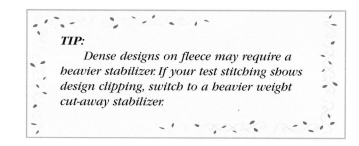

TIP:
Dense designs on fleece may require a heavier stabilizer. If your test stitching shows design clipping, switch to a heavier weight cut-away stabilizer.

GENERAL STATEMENT:
On fill-stitched motifs, if your test-stitching shows bits of fleece peeking between the stitches, and loosening the tension does not correct the problem, a topping is warranted. Refer to Chapter 1 for more information about toppings.

Combining Designs

To add a bit more interest to the solitary Fern, overlay it onto the Frayed Patch (see page 28). Use a heavier weight stabilizer (or two layers of lighter stabilizer) to handle stitching both designs.

Embroider the Frayed Patch first, using a thread color slightly darker than your fleece (or a subtle metallic). After the Frayed Patch is stitched, load the Fern onto your machine. Stitch the Fern over the Frayed Patch. Center or offset the Fern according to your taste.

Fern

The Fern may be a bit dense for lightweight fleeces. If your test-stitch sample puckers, increase the design size 10% to 20%, add another layer of stabilizer and test-stitch again. Or, keep the design as is and add another layer of cut-away stabilizer for added stability.

Clustered Leaves

The Clustered Leaves design can provide a subtle embroidery embellishment when you just want to add a little something for interest. A few clusters tossed randomly on a denim shirt would be very attractive.

Embossed

Stamping and embossing are popular looks in fashion and home dec. We can accomplish this understated look with embroidery by using the functional underlay stitches as decorative stitches. Stitch segment 3 (underlay) in a thread color slightly darker than your fleece or with a variegated thread. Try stitching segment 4 alone for a mottled stamp accent.

Etched

For a motif with a little more definition, stitch just the outline and detail veins of the design, segments 2 and 6.

Trapunto

It seems like Trapunto can be used with just about every design that has an outline stitch. Add subtle depth to the Etched technique by including a layer of batting between the stabilizer and the base fleece, then stitch only segment 2. For more information, refer to Trapunto with Batting (Stippled Flower) instructions on page 20.

Combining Designs

The Textured Frame design on page 28 in the New Concepts chapter offers the opportunity to frame the leaves. Load the Clustered Leaves design onto your machine and reduce the design 10% to 20%. Stitch segments 1, 2, 5 and 6 (leaves outline and detail). Load the Textured Frame onto your machine and enlarge the design 10% to 20% to just clear the perimeter of the leaves. Stitch segment 3 (frame).

Fir Tree

The Fir Tree is a fun design with a variety of elements to pick and choose. The options are many and the results are very different. If you stitch the Fir Tree "as intended" you have a lovely, realistic and stitch-filled tree with wispy edges and etched highlights. Use multiples for a mini forest or combine the tree with other designs for a scenic landscape.

Stitched "as intended," it may be too dense for use on lightweight fleece without added stabilization. But, the "hidden designs" offer you a variety of effects without using the entire design.

Blunt Edge Appliqué

Depending on how much or how little detail you want, pick and choose a variety of stitch segments to accent your appliqué. Stitch segment 1 (perimeter baste) to secure the fleece appliqué piece onto your base fleece. Then, stitch any of the following combinations: segments 2 & 6, 5 & 6, 6 & 7, or 6 alone. For more information, refer to Blunt Edge Appliqué instructions (Rocking Horse) on page 10.

Trapunto I

Stitch segment 2 (outline). Insert stuffing and finish with segment 6. Stuff lightly and handle gently so that the finishing stitches align properly. Change to a larger needle to handle the added bulk of the stuffing. For more information, refer to Trapunto instructions (Southwest Star) on page 18.

Trapunto II

When the designs came back from the digitizer, I immediately fell in love with segment 5 all by itself. I just had to see if I could "Trapunto" when there wasn't a complete outline. It worked! For more information, refer to Trapunto with Batting instructions (Stippled Flower) on page 20.

Textured

Here's another instance where one segment of stitching alone provides an attractive stitch effect. The stitches compress the fleece, resulting in an "embossed" tree and the uneven stitched lines look like branches. Stitch segment 4.

Combining Designs

The simple snowflakes not only offer a scenic background for the tree but a great element to use as a frame. Stitch segment 7 (the snowflakes). Mirror image the design and then stitch only the snowflakes again. You have a great "frame" for other motifs!

Ladybug

As is the case with many fill-stitch designs, the Ladybug is great stitched on woven fabrics. However, it may be a little too dense for use on fleece without added stabilization. Again, look at all the "hidden designs" that offer great potential for other techniques.

"Dot" Options

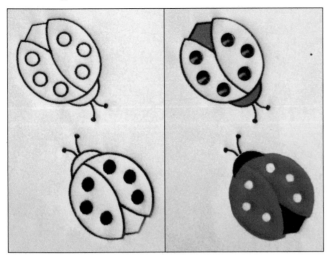

The dots alone, offer the Ladybug numerous "fashion choices." Dress up the wings by using one of the following ideas:

- Dramatic outlined dots: Stitch segments 4 and 10 (outline and satin stitch)
- Filled dots: Stitch segments 4 and 5 (outline and fill) optional 10 (satin stitch finish)
- Overlaid outline stitched dots with shiny black size 20 (1/2") sport snaps!
- Reverse Appliqué: Stitch segment 4 (outline) . Dots left "unfilled" and top fleece layer trimmed away to reveal the base fleece.

Blunt Edge & Reverse Appliqué Combination

This combination is fun — Blunt Edge Appliqué wings with reverse appliqué dots. Refer to Blunt Edge Appliqué instructions (Rocking Horse) on page 10, and Reverse Appliqué instructions (Contemporary Cat) on page 12.

Instructions:

1. Lay a piece of contrasting fleece for the appliqué over the base fleece. Stitch segments 2 and 4 (wings and dots outline). Remove hoop from machine. Trim excess fleece appliqué close to outer edges of wings. (Do not trim dots.)

2. Replace hoop on machine and stitch segments 6, 7, and 8 (body outline & fill, antennae segments).

3. Trim away the top fleece layer inside the dots (to reveal the base fleece color.)

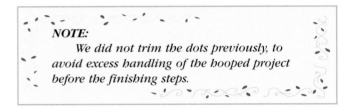

NOTE:
We did not trim the dots previously, to avoid excess handling of the hooped project before the finishing steps.

Trapunto

Trapunto provides us with a "pleasingly plump" ladybug and lends a totally different flavor to this design. Stitch segment 2 (wings outline) and insert stuffing. Change to a larger needle and finish with segments 4, 6, 8, 9, and 10 (everything except the fill stitched wings and dots). The end result is a ladybug with lofty wings and recessed dots. For more information, refer to Trapunto instructions (Southwest Star) on page 18.

Elegant Snowflake

This simple, yet elegant snowflake motif is a prime example of a design that offers so much more than initially meets the eye. At first glance, all you see is a monochromatic design with a simple satin stitch framing the motif. But, this simple design breaks down into many "hidden designs"!

Blunt Edge Appliqué

Blunt Edge Appliqué takes on completely different looks depending upon which segments you choose. Three possibilities are: Stitch segment 2 (outline). Stitch segment 2 and 3 (outline inner and outer motif). Or, stitch segments 2, 3, and half of segment 5 (inner and outer outlines and the underlay portion of segment 5). For more information, refer to Blunt Edge Appliqué instructions (Rocking Horse) on page 10.

Reverse Appliqué

The outer perimeter stitches are good choices for reverse appliqué. Stitch segment 2 (outline), segments 2 and 5 (satin stitched outline), or segment 2 and half of segment 5 (outline and underlay portion of segment 5). For more information, refer to Reverse Appliqué instructions (Contemporary Cat) on page 12.

Textured

Any combination of segments, stitched directly onto the base fleece creates texture from the sunken stitches. Try stitching segment 2 alone (outline), segment 3 alone (inner motif outline), and segments 2 and 3 alone (inner and outer outline).

Or, experiment with: segments 2, 3, and half of 5 (inner and outer outlines and underlay portion of 5), segment 2 with a double needle (outline), or half of segment 5 with a double needle (underlay portion of 5).

Trapunto

Stitch segment 2 (outline) and insert stuffing, or stitch segment 2 (outline) and insert a little bit of stuffing and finish with segment 3 (inner motif outline). Try stitching segment 2 (outline) using a double needle and then insert stuffing. For more information, refer to Trapunto instructions (Southwest Star) on page 18.

Crystal Snowflake

This crystalline snowflake is dramatic when stitched with the satin stitches, delicate when stitched using only the outline stitches, and versatile when broken apart like the Nested Flowers.

Textured

Stitch segments 2, 4, 6, 8, and 10 (outlines) using a contrasting thread (for more visibility), or a color slightly darker than the fleece (for subtlety).

Trapunto

The Crystal Snowflake offers the same options as the Nested Flower on page 23. Stitch segments 2, 8 and 10 for the Trapunto effect pictured. Or, use any of the segments to create Blunt Edge Appliqué, Double- Sided Appliqué, Reverse Appliqué, Chenille, Double Needle, or Dimensional Appliqué!

Large Framed Leaves and Small Framed Leaf

I'm covering both of these designs together, because the designs have so much in common. I had fun creating these designs. I love the simplicity of the leaves and the embossed look of the wood grain textured ground. Stitched "as is," the Large Framed Leaves offer subtle embellishment to any fleece project. The fill stitched Small Framed Leaf offers the additional opportunity to "paint" with dramatic autumn colors. I especially had fun visualizing all the "hidden designs" both designs have to offer.

Blunt Edge Appliqué

If you want only one blunt edge appliquéd leaf, use the Small Framed Leaf design. If you want a pair of leaves, use the Large Framed Leaves. If you want realism, embellish your project with a mixture of single and double leaves. Stitch the outline and the vein detail (segments 4 and 5 for the double leaves; segments 4 and 10 for the single leaf) and trim the excess appliqué. For more information, refer to Blunt Edge Appliqué instructions (Rocking Horse) on page 10.

Double-Sided Appliqué

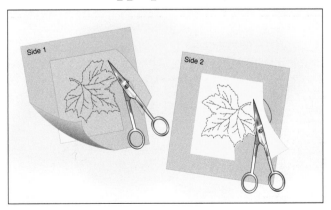

Double-sided appliqué is a great technique for making fabulous blankets and scarves. This technique allows you to enjoy both sides of the project. As with the Blunt Edge Appliqué above, choose the single leaf from the Small Framed Leaf, the double leaves from the Large Framed Leaves, or a combination of both. Use a contrast color fleece for the leaves, and stitch the outline and vein detail (segments 4 and 5 for the double leaves; segments 4 and 10 for the single leaf) and trim the excess appliqué. Scatter leaves on a blanket or cascade leaves down a scarf. For more information, refer to Double-Sided Appliqué instructions (Rocking Horse) on page 10.

Trapunto

Use the Large Framed Leaves to stitch segment 2 (background) and segment 4 (leaf outline), insert stuffing, and finish the leaves with the vein detail (segment 5 for the double leaves; segment 10 for the single leaf). Change to a larger size needle to stitch the veins. For more information, refer to Trapunto instructions (Southwest Star) on page 18.

Double Needle Embroidery

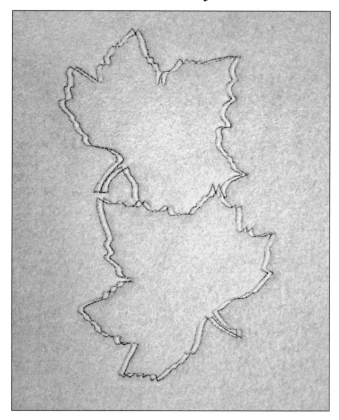

If one needle is good, then two must be better! Stitch just segment 4 (leaf outline) using a 3.0 double needle.

The underside of double needle stitching is fabulous! The threads are forced to the back side of the fabric providing a cord effect. Embroider in reverse with the stabilizer on top and the fleece next to the bed of the machine. Hoop lightly by loosening the hoop screws dramatically. Stitch just the leaf outlines (segment 4) using a 3.0 double needle.

Textured

For an etched look, choose a thread color slightly darker than your fleece or a subtle variegated thread and stitch segments 4, 5, and 10 of the Small Framed Leaf.

For a textured appearance, stitch only segment 2 (background) of the Small Framed Leaf with a variegated thread. It would be fun to sprinkle the textured background on a solid color fleece to create a subtle all-over print.

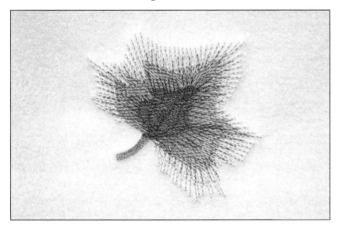

The stitching of the first part of segment 6, and all of segments 7 and 8 offers a "smudged" detail of the leaves. Use these elements alone or in combination with other segments.

Project Ideas

Snowflake Scarf

The Crystal Snowflake produces a gorgeous accent for the edge of a fleece scarf. The scarf will be visible on both sides, so each side of the snowflake will need to be pretty. Using a heavy weight water-soluble stabilizer and decorative thread in the bobbin will accomplish our purpose.

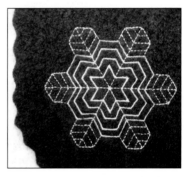

Instructions:

1. Place the decorative thread both in the bobbin and through the needle.
2. Hoop a heavy weight water-soluble stabilizer.
3. Slightly dampen the stabilizer with a sponge to make it tacky.
4. Adhere the edge of the scarf to the stabilizer and stitch the motif.
5. Rinse the stabilizer away following the manufacturer's directions.

Autumn Pullover

Ladybug Jumpsuit

The graduated colors in this gorgeous fleece provide a wonderful canvas for the Small Framed Leaf design. By skipping the fill stitch segments, you have an airy leaf motif that does not overpower the fleece. Variegated thread compliments the ombre coloration. The directions for the Polar Ribbing neckline finish can be found in *Polar Magic*.

The adorable Ladybug provides a quick way to add embellishment when the wings are stitched using the Blunt Edge Appliqué technique. Simply layer, stitch and trim! The dots can be finished in a variety of ways — reverse appliqué, satin stitch outline, fill stitches, sport snaps, or buttons.

Pillow Sampler

Two-Tone Tunic

The versatile Fir Tree offers a great opportunity to create a pillow sampler. The first tree (upper left) is stitched "complete" whereas the rest of the trees are stitched using the "hidden designs." The second tree (upper right) features Trapunto using batting and segment 5. The third tree (lower left) features stuffed Trapunto using segments 2 and 6. The wispy last tree (lower right) was embroidered using segment 4. Directions for the Fat Piping pillow finish can be found in *Polar Magic*.

The Elegant Snowflake makes a great tunic sampler when you can't decide on which technique you like the best. Use a variety of the "hidden designs" this motif has to offer. If you want stronger royal color snowflakes stitched on white fleece, use two strands of decorative thread through a 90/14 needle. If subtlety is more your style, double-up using white decorative thread for the snowflakes on the royal fleece. Directions for creating the double-needle Polar Ribbing neckline finish can be found in *Polar Magic*.

Spectacular Blanket

Tumbling leaves on both sides of this blanket make it "right side up" no matter how it is tossed on the couch. For variety, choose different color leaves for each side of the blanket. The Double-Sided Appliqué technique

makes the project easy. Use the Small Framed Leaf in a large hoop, enlarged 20%, and stitch segments 4 and 10. Engage the mirror image and rotation function on your embroidery machine to create realistic leaves falling at various angles. The "yarn" finish is made from strips of fleece laced around a wave bade rotary cut blanket edge.

Laced edge-finish

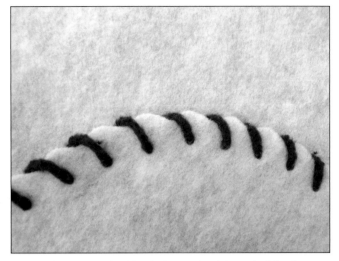

This is a lovely finish for a double-sided leaf appliqué blanket or scarf. Make your own "fleece yarn" to coordinate with the leaves.

Instructions:

1. Cut a strip of contrast fleece on the cross-grain (direction of most stretch) exactly 3/8" wide X 60" long. Cut off both selvages. Grab one end of the fleece strip and pull the strip between pinched fingers, stretching the fleece tightly. The fleece will curl and form a yarn.

2. Using a wave blade, rotary cut all four edges of your scarf or blanket.

3. Thread fleece yarn through the large eye of a tapestry needle and "lace" the blanket or scarf edges by wrapping the yarn around the edge. Use the wave cuts as a spacing guide. Tie fleece yarn together for longer pieces, as needed.

Now that you've reached the end of the book, my hope is that you'll look at the designs you own (and all those you plan to purchase) with a new appreciation. Look for all the "hidden designs" that can be utilized for fleece and other surface embellishments. Explore and have fun!

Clustered Leaves   Stitch Count: 12,831   Size: 3.43" x 3.41" (87.2mm x 86.6mm)

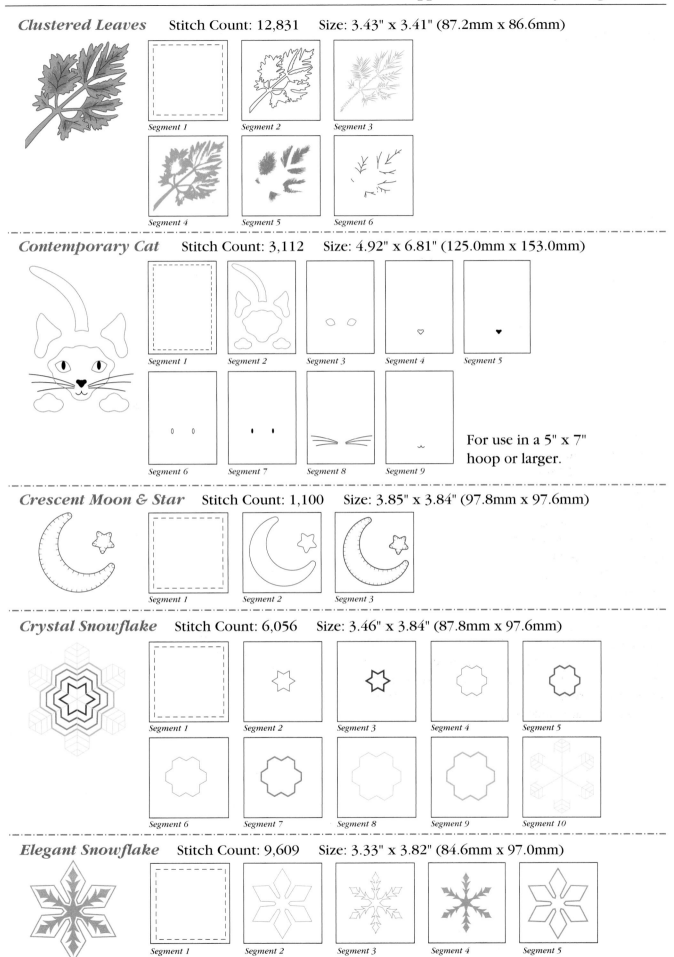

Segment 1   *Segment 2*   *Segment 3*
Segment 4   *Segment 5*   *Segment 6*

Contemporary Cat   Stitch Count: 3,112   Size: 4.92" x 6.81" (125.0mm x 153.0mm)

Segment 1   *Segment 2*   *Segment 3*   *Segment 4*   *Segment 5*
Segment 6   *Segment 7*   *Segment 8*   *Segment 9*

For use in a 5" x 7" hoop or larger.

Crescent Moon & Star   Stitch Count: 1,100   Size: 3.85" x 3.84" (97.8mm x 97.6mm)

Segment 1   *Segment 2*   *Segment 3*

Crystal Snowflake   Stitch Count: 6,056   Size: 3.46" x 3.84" (87.8mm x 97.6mm)

Segment 1   *Segment 2*   *Segment 3*   *Segment 4*   *Segment 5*
Segment 6   *Segment 7*   *Segment 8*   *Segment 9*   *Segment 10*

Elegant Snowflake   Stitch Count: 9,609   Size: 3.33" x 3.82" (84.6mm x 97.0mm)

Segment 1   *Segment 2*   *Segment 3*   *Segment 4*   *Segment 5*

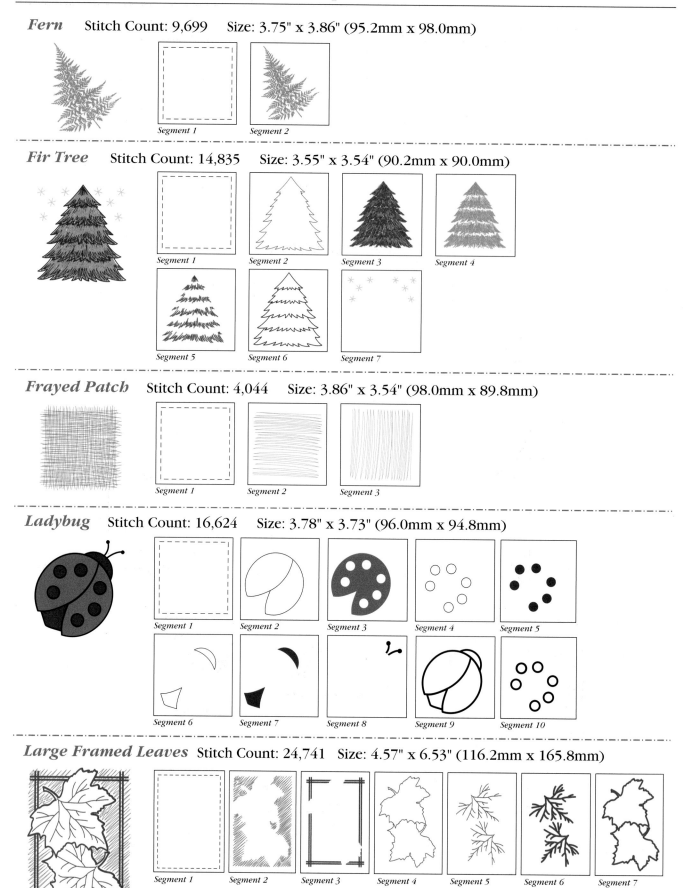

Fern   Stitch Count: 9,699   Size: 3.75" x 3.86" (95.2mm x 98.0mm)

Segment 1   *Segment 2*

Fir Tree   Stitch Count: 14,835   Size: 3.55" x 3.54" (90.2mm x 90.0mm)

Segment 1   *Segment 2*   *Segment 3*   *Segment 4*

Segment 5   *Segment 6*   *Segment 7*

Frayed Patch   Stitch Count: 4,044   Size: 3.86" x 3.54" (98.0mm x 89.8mm)

Segment 1   *Segment 2*   *Segment 3*

Ladybug   Stitch Count: 16,624   Size: 3.78" x 3.73" (96.0mm x 94.8mm)

Segment 1   *Segment 2*   *Segment 3*   *Segment 4*   *Segment 5*

Segment 6   *Segment 7*   *Segment 8*   *Segment 9*   *Segment 10*

Large Framed Leaves   Stitch Count: 24,741   Size: 4.57" x 6.53" (116.2mm x 165.8mm)

Segment 1   *Segment 2*   *Segment 3*   *Segment 4*   *Segment 5*   *Segment 6*   *Segment 7*

For use in a 5" x 7" hoop or larger.

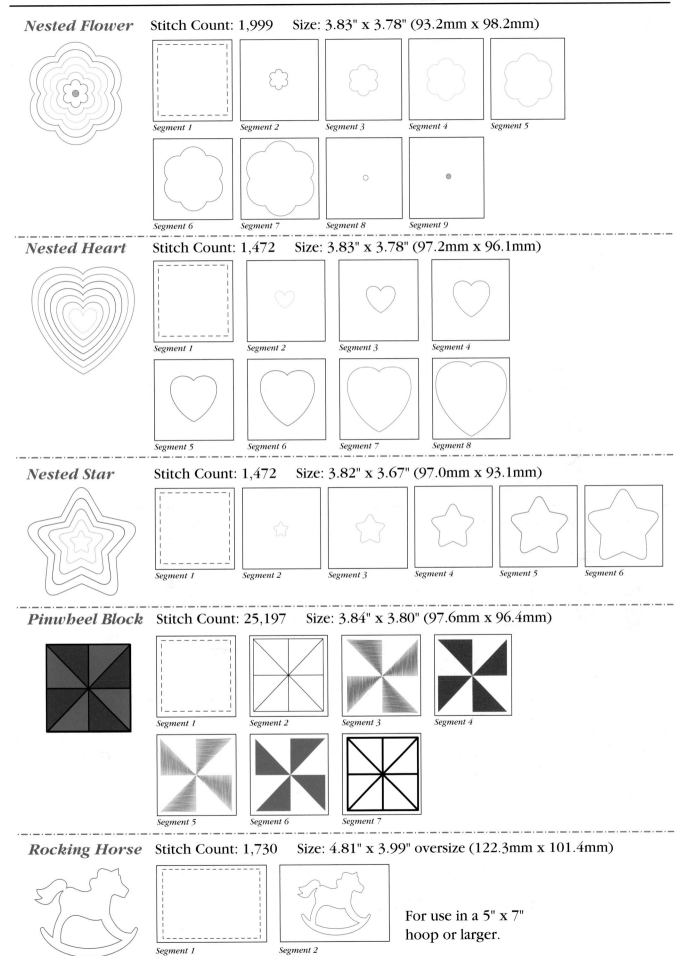

Nested Flower   Stitch Count: 1,999   Size: 3.83" x 3.78" (93.2mm x 98.2mm)

Segment 1   Segment 2   Segment 3   Segment 4   Segment 5

Segment 6   Segment 7   Segment 8   Segment 9

Nested Heart   Stitch Count: 1,472   Size: 3.83" x 3.78" (97.2mm x 96.1mm)

Segment 1   Segment 2   Segment 3   Segment 4

Segment 5   Segment 6   Segment 7   Segment 8

Nested Star   Stitch Count: 1,472   Size: 3.82" x 3.67" (97.0mm x 93.1mm)

Segment 1   Segment 2   Segment 3   Segment 4   Segment 5   Segment 6

Pinwheel Block   Stitch Count: 25,197   Size: 3.84" x 3.80" (97.6mm x 96.4mm)

Segment 1   Segment 2   Segment 3   Segment 4

Segment 5   Segment 6   Segment 7

Rocking Horse   Stitch Count: 1,730   Size: 4.81" x 3.99" oversize (122.3mm x 101.4mm)

Segment 1   Segment 2

For use in a 5" x 7"
hoop or larger.

Small Framed Leaf   Stitch Count: 23,627   Size: 3.84" x 3.90" (97.6mm x 99.0mm)

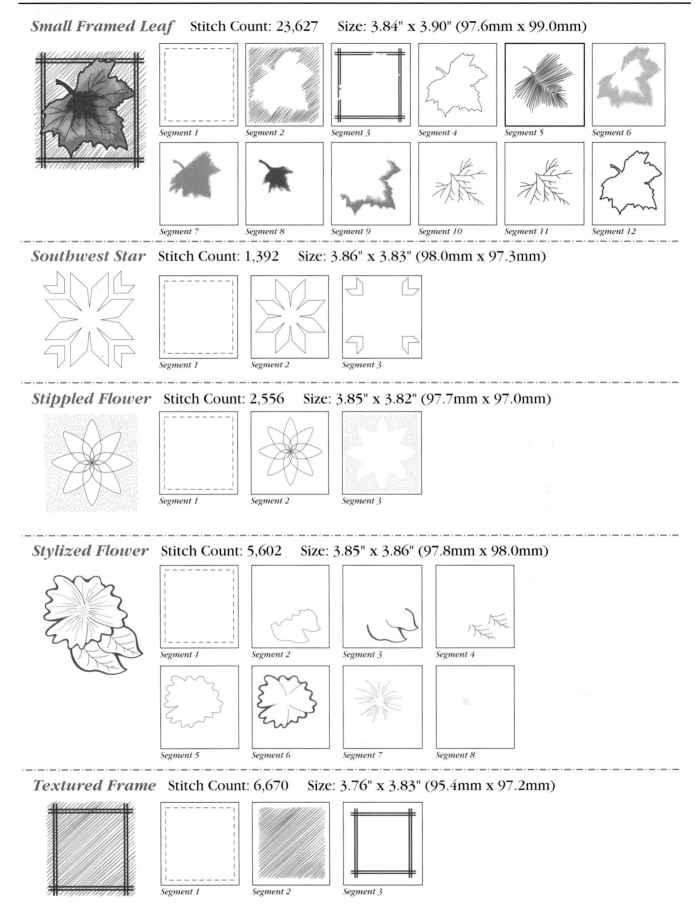

Segment 1   Segment 2   Segment 3   Segment 4   Segment 5   Segment 6

Segment 7   Segment 8   Segment 9   Segment 10   Segment 11   Segment 12

Southwest Star   Stitch Count: 1,392   Size: 3.86" x 3.83" (98.0mm x 97.3mm)

Segment 1   Segment 2   Segment 3

Stippled Flower   Stitch Count: 2,556   Size: 3.85" x 3.82" (97.7mm x 97.0mm)

Segment 1   Segment 2   Segment 3

Stylized Flower   Stitch Count: 5,602   Size: 3.85" x 3.86" (97.8mm x 98.0mm)

Segment 1   Segment 2   Segment 3   Segment 4

Segment 5   Segment 6   Segment 7   Segment 8

Textured Frame   Stitch Count: 6,670   Size: 3.76" x 3.83" (95.4mm x 97.2mm)

Segment 1   Segment 2   Segment 3

Resources

Look for these and other embroidery-related products at your local retailer where embroidery products are sold. Visit www.embroideryresource.com for a comprehensive listing of embroidery machine products.

Embroidery Machine Companies

Baby Lock USA
Call 1-800-422-2952 for a dealer near you.
www.babylock.com

Bernina of America
Call 1-800-405-2739 for a dealer near you.
www.berninausa.com

Brother International
Call 1-800-422-7684 for a dealer near you.
www.brother.com
www.brothermall.com

Elna USA
Call 1-800-848-3562 for a dealer near you.
www.elnausa.com

Viking Sewing Machines
Call 1-800-358-0001 for a dealer near you.
www.husqvarnaviking.com

Janome America
Call 1-800-631-0183 for a dealer near you.
www.janome.com

Kenmore
Call 1-847-758-0900
www.sears.com

Pfaff American Sales Corp.
Call 1-800-997-3233 for a dealer near you.
www.pfaffusa.com

Simplicity
Call 1-800-553-5332
www.simplicitysewing.com

Singer Company
Call 1-800-474-6437 for a dealer near you.
www.singerco.com

Embroidery Design Companies

Cactus Punch
Call 1-520-622-8460 for a dealer near you.
www.cactuspunch.com

Criswell Embroidery
Call 1-800-308-5442 for a dealer near you.
www.k-lace.com

Dakota Collectibles
Call 1-800-331-3160 for a dealer near you.
www.dakotacollectibles.com

Embroideryarts
Call 1-888-238-1372 for a dealer near you.
www.embroideryarts.com

Martha Pullen
Call 1-800-547-4176 for a dealer near you.
www.marthapullen.com

Oklahoma Embroidery Supply & Design (OESD)
See your local sewing & embroidery dealer.
Call 1-800-580-8885
www.embroideryonline.com

Sudberry House
1-860-739-6951
www.machinecrossstitch.com
www.sudberry.com

Suzanne Hinshaw
1-407-323-8706
www.suzannehinshaw.com

Vermillion Stitchery
1-949-452-0155
www.vsccs.com

Recommended Reading

For more information on sewing and creativity with fleece, refer to Nancy Cornwell's books: *Adventures with Polarfleece®, More Polarfleece® Adventures,* and *Polar Magic.*

For more fleece embroidery designs, refer to Nancy Cornwell's Cactus Punch *Signature Series Disk #45 — Adventures with Fleece.*

For more information on embroidery, refer to Jeanine Twigg's books: *Embroidery Machine Essentials,* and her *Project Companion Series: Basic Techniques.*

CD-ROM Instructions

The embroidery designs featured in this book are located on the CD-ROM. You must have a computer and compatible embroidery software to access and utilize the decorative designs. Basic computer knowledge is helpful to understand how to copy the designs onto the hard drive of your computer.

To access the designs, insert the CD into your computer. The designs are located on the CD in folders for each embroidery machine format. Copy the design files onto the hard drive of your computer or open the design in applicable embroidery software. Be sure to copy only the design format compatible with your brand of embroidery equipment.

Once the designs are in your embroidery software or saved on your computer, transfer the designs to your embroidery machine following the manufacturer's instructions for the equipment. For more information about using these designs with your software or embroidery equipment, consult your owner's manual or seek advice from the dealer that honors your equipment warranty.

Full-size images of each design with smaller images of the individual segments are included on the CD in PDF (Portable Document Format) format files. In addition, the Appendix: Design Detail (pages 43 - 46) is on the CD for your convenience. Utilize these pages for design templates and thread color choices.

You will need Adobe Acrobat Reader 5.0 or higher to view and print these files. The CD includes the latest version of this software for your convenience.